UNMASKING
THE REAL ME

By
Nakeeta
McNeil

Unmasking the Real Me
Copyright © 2020 Nakeeta McNeil

All rights reserved.

No part of this book may be reproduced or transmitted in any form or by any means, electronic or mechanical, including photocopying, recording or by any information storage and retrieval system, without written permission from the author, except for the inclusion of brief quotations in a review.

Address inquiries to the publisher:

3741 Riverside Drive, Unit A
Coral Springs, FL 33065

ISBN: 978-1-7355723-0-7 (Print)
ISBN: 978-1-7355723-1-4 (Ebook)

Library of Congress Control Number: 2020916266

Editor: Annette R. Johnson

Printed in the United States of America

CONTENTS

ACKNOWLEDGEMENTS

I would like to express my appreciation to the many people who stood by me over the years and did not give up on me even though I wasn't the most friendly individual to deal with at times.

I would like to thank Pastor Natalee Pryce for all her Sunday School and mentor encouragement. That kept me from sin, even on the days it seemed impossible to do so. It was quotes like "sit under it" that helped me through.

Most of all, I would like to thank my mom for giving birth to me and believing in me every step of the way, even though I gave her a lot of trouble growing up and even still a little today. Thanks to my brother, Jahvain Grant, who came after me the day I decided to run away even though he was sick.

I would like to thank my grandparents, Icyline Wiggan and Clinton Wiggan, for whooping my behind and straighten me back up when I would act out of character as a child.

I would like to thank Elder Pryce for helping me through the process of selection, encouragement and graphic design preparation for my book.

Thanks to Michelle Boswell for opening her home to me and for being like a second mom in my life. In addition, words can't explain how much I appreciate and thank my spiritual mom, Apostle Sonia Lee. She is the one who labored in prayer and believed God for me. Thanks for never giving up on me even when others did, and thanks for the never-ending encouragement of what a powerful Woman of God I am. Most importantly, thanks for reminding me that all I have to do is "let go and let God."

And last but definitely not least, I apologize to all those names I failed to mention who have touched my life in one way or another throughout this journey.

CHAPTER 1

Proving Them Wrong

It all started when I was 12 years old. I started to see life more clearly then.

My grandmother was calling me from the kitchen.

"Yes, mama," I answered.

"Your mom is on the phone, and she would like to talk to you."

"Hi, mummy," I said after taking the phone from my grandmother. "When are you coming back for me? I'm tired of living here. Everything is so hard, and I know America is a much better place for me to live."

I got straight to the point. It was like I was holding it in for a long time and couldn't wait for the first opportunity to tell her.

"Well, baby, I don›t have the money right now, and I still didn't get my papers to travel yet," she told me.

I was so upset that I told her I was going to kill myself because I was counting on her to make everything better and do it right away. My grandmother took the phone away from me and made it clear to me that I was not going to kill her first daughter with stress. "Do you want my daughter to go strip to make money? Not over her dead body," she continued.

I disrespectfully rolled my eyes and stormed out the living room mumbling.

I'm not one who likes to be told what to do, and for that matter, I sometimes find myself in tense situations that are difficult for me to escape and manage. Even when I have gotten out of these situations, I would find myself back down that same road again because I didn›t learn the first time.

I was a very serious child growing up. I was not very peaceful and humble. I was the one in my household that was ready to curse people out and fight for the least little thing so I could show them how big and bad I was.

I came from a Christian background as far as I can remember, but why do I have to get baptized? I thought to myself. Everywhere I went, people wanted to tell me about God, but I wasn't interested in all the religious stuff.

My grandmother forced me to go to church every Sunday. The church I attended was about a 15-minute walk from my grandmother's house in Hanover, Jamaica. I didn't know how to drive, so I had to walk or get a ride wherever I needed to go. The one time I ever remembered driving was when I was much younger and almost drove my dad's car in a river. The funny thing about that day was that I was only 9 years old and the legal age to drive was 18. I was so scared. I promised myself I would never try to drive another car again.

I walked to church every Sunday morning, and as rebellious as I was, the one thing that I always looked forward to was praise and worship. The three young women who sang on the praise team were my friends, but every time I told them that I wanted to sing with them, they would laugh at me. They felt I wouldn't be able to harmonize with them in order to sing on the praise team.

Our pastor had preached on the scripture "I can do all things through Christ that strengthens me," so I felt I could eventually sing with them if I practiced. I thought about what they said to me and at that point in my life, I decided to prove them wrong. In fact, I felt that whatever they would do, I could do better.

CHAPTER 2

Learning Lessons

I started writing poems until one day I found myself singing them. I would sometimes imagine myself as Beyonce or Ciara on stage. My bed was the stage and the broomstick was the microphone.

My Aunt Crissy was more of a sister to me. I don't have a biological sister, so I shared everything with her, even my food sometimes. I was in my bedroom singing when she walked in and asked, "What are you singing, girl?"

"I wrote it," I told her.

However, she didn't believe me at first, so she asked, "So, really you wrote it?"

I just gave her a look without saying a word.

"It sounds really good," she added.

"Thank you," I said. "So do you think that I could be a bigtime artist one day?"

"Of course, girl, but just don't forget me when you make it big time." She added, "Here's a word of advice for you, my niece. Never stop writing until you've touched everyone that God will have you to touch through the words or lyrics of your songs however way you do it. I don't really understand the whole music thing. Give me a front desk position in a hotel, and I am in a world by myself."

The thing that was puzzling about what she said to me was about who God wanted me to touch. It was really funny because since she got baptized, she never went back to church. However, now here she was giving me advice based on God. I thought, "Oh man, this is why I always spend my offering, which my grandmother always gave me for Sunday School, at the shop down the street because if my aunt wasn't doing the whole church thing, why should I?" Plus, my friend Kim told me that if I got baptized and all, that it meant good-bye to drinking and parties. I loved to party, so I thought maybe when I get older, I will serve God with my whole heart, but for now, praise and worship was going to have to do.

My church hosted Vacation Bible School every summer for the kids who stayed back in the community when the schools were on summer break. It was something that the youths looked forward to attending. From making certificates to creating gift boxes, there was something for every age group. If you couldn't sing, you could dance or take turns teaching a class. It was during Vacation Bible School that I learned a few Scriptures I could quote.

CHAPTER 3

Finding a Father Figure

I got my first job at the age of 13. I would listen to this Christian radio station called VYBZ 96.3 FM. On Sundays, the station hosted a kid's program where you could call in and quote a Bible verses and explain what it meant to you. I decided to try it one Sunday with one of the scriptures I already knew. I chose John 3:16, which state, "For God so loved the world that he gave His only begotten son that whosoever believeth in him should not perish but have everlasting life."

I told the host, whose name was Michael Hyper, that what I got from that scripture is that God really does love me, and if I believed his Word, then everything else will fall in place. I continued doing it for like three months every Sunday morning until one morning when I called in, I got offered a job over the air to work at the radio station on Saturdays with DJ Toni and DJ Rocky. I was so excited when he asked me the question that I didn't even think about it. I said yes without any hesitation. It was the best decision I ever made. I got a chance to work with other kids, and even though I was the oldest, I still felt like I was a part of their family. I grew a close relationship with my boss, and he became like a father figure in my life. I was like a daughter to him since he didn't have any children.

CHAPTER 4

Memory Lane

Growing up wasn't always easy. I wasn't raised by my mom and dad. My father lived in Jamaica, but it was like I didn't have a dad. He lived 20 minutes away from me, but sometimes it took him almost a year before I would hear from or see him. I knew he didn't have it financially to give me material things, but that wasn't what I was lacking. It was his love and his mere presence. He was absent through much of my youth. I thank God for my grandparents who held it together through thick and thin.

I can remember times I had to go without new or updated clothing like other kids and food, not knowing where the next meal was coming from. The struggle was so real that I literally felt it in my stomach every day. As a result, I hung with the wrong crowd just to fit in and get a sense of belonging. I would skip school with my two friends and go to boys' house to drink and smoke on a daily basis. I would back talk my grandparents, and I partied like there was no tomorrow. I would go to a party at like 10 p.m. and go back home at 4 a.m. the next day.

My grandparents would try to beat this one scripture in my head every time I decided to act out of character: "Submit to God, resist the devil, and he will flee from you" (James 4:7). Still, no matter how many times my grandparents would beat me, I still wouldn't change. In my opinion, my school was to be blame because the staff there sold us liquor and the administrators allowed us to wear clothes that made us practically look naked.

In addition, our neighborhood wasn't very peaceful on a daily basis. My family owned the land that we lived on, and my great grandparents were very caring and sharing. They allowed another family to live on a portion of our land. If they were still alive today, I think they would have regretted their decision to let those people live on our land because as the years went by, the family started to invade other places on our land. Our family's own personal boundaries and space were no longer respected over time. Plus, their kids were unruly and mischievous. They would plot traps and mess around with my uncle so he would get hurt.

I would never forget this particular situation that took place when I was a child. My grandparents had planted their corn, tomatoes and lettuce, and it was time for them to harvest. The crops would be ready in another week or so. I was in my bedroom when I heard tractors in the backyard. I yelled for my grandparents to come and see the disaster I was witnessing. I started crying because I couldn't believe that a set of people could be so heartless.

It was one thing for their kids to mess with my uncle, but they had really crossed the line by destroying the crops. I couldn't understand why my grandparents were so calm about the situation. They just kept on telling me that everything was going to be okay because they knew the God that they served and never fails.

CHAPTER 5

Preparing for Departure

My mom was finally returned to Jamaica when I was 14 and my brother, Jahvain, was 11. We were so excited that we wanted to go meet her at the airport. The car was not big enough to fit everyone, so we waited at home.

When she arrived, we both ran, hugged her, and told her how happy we were to finally see her again. The truth was we really wanted to see what she bought for us from the United States so we could show them off to our friends. However, my mom had other plans. Turns out, she was there on strictly business to get us to America.

The next day, we had to get up early in the morning. I really could not understand why, but I got up anyways. My brother was usually the last to get up, but even he woke up on time. We got on the first bus on its way to the embassy in Kingston.

When we got there, we sat outside underneath a tent. My mom started to coach me and brother on how we need to "look those people in their eyes" when we were answering each question and smile. I started thinking what if we don't get our green card because of me because I broke myself in the habit of not smiling because of the environment in which I lived. I would watch the guys in my neighborhood, even the older ones, and how they approached girls. Just because the girls were laughing with them, the guys took it as a sign of weakness to take advantage of the young girls. This even happened in the churches, too. One of the many reasons I didn't commit to any churches was because they were all hypocrites in my eyes.

Turns out, I went so far down memory lane that my mom had been calling me for the past minute and I didn't even hear her. It was our time to go in for an immigration interview. When we got to the glass partition with a white lady on the other side, she questioned my mother first, then my brother, and finally, it was my turn. To make sure I followed my mother's instructions, I smiled broadly, showing most all my teeth, for every question.

It was a two-day process, which meant we had to stay in town until the next day. We stayed with one of my mom's friend for the night. The next morning, I got up and prayed, asking God to come through for us that day. Before we left the house, my mom took out a bottle of olive oil and started rubbing it on me and my brother. That made me kind of mad because I was smelling like cooking oil. I got over it by the time we got to the embassy, though. It was definitely our day. The embassy people did not ask us any other questions.

They just handed us our green cards among other official documents and assured us that we were eligible to become residents of the United States. We were so hopeful and excited. It was unexplainable.

CHAPTER 6

Good-Bye, Jamaica.
Hello, America.

Two weeks later, after many good-byes, the day finally arrived. The day had come when I would no longer be living in Jamaica, and I would be living in America. We packed all that was useful to travel. Unlike other kids who, perhaps, would travel with their two to three suitcases, my brother and I could only travel with a little bag because that's all our mom could afford.

My grandparents were crying and I was trying to convince them that this is not like the other times when they would grow family members kids and they grew up to forget the good that they did for them. I would never forget where I came from, especially how half the time when mangoes, among other fresh fruit, were what my grandmother and I had to sell to make ends meet. Even on holidays, when my brother and my cousins would go off to their individual family members, I was always the one who stayed with my grandparents. Everything they taught me made me the woman I am today.

After finally getting my grandparents to stop crying, we

said our final good-byes and headed out to the airport. Our flight was scheduled for later on that day, so while we were at the airport, we got something to eat because my mother told us that only first class passengers get real food on the plane. All other passengers get peanuts and juice, so we were going to have to eat Burger King. I looked at my brother and my brother was looking at me. We shook our head in comparison. In our minds, we didn't care if we had to eat crackers as long as we made it to America safely.

By the time we got done eating, went to the restroom and walked around a little, it was time for us to start boarding our plane. "Now boarding Flight…," I will never forget this moment. We started running toward the gate before the lady on the speaker could say the flight number. When we got to the airport security checkpoint, we had to remove all our jewelry and walk through some sort of a scanner door to check for anything that was not acceptable on the plane. After going through that procedure, we walked to the departure gate and had to take our seat on the airplane.

"Attention, all passengers, everyone should now be seated to prepare for takeoff," said a flight attendant holding a microphone who stood near the cockpit. One of the other flight attendants was walking down the aisle to demonstrate the safety and evacuation instructions should there be an emergency. Then the pilot finally said what I had dreamed about time after time before, "We are now getting ready for takeoff."

The next stop was Fort Lauderdale, Florida, airport. When

the airplane took off from the runway, my exact words were: "Good-bye, Jamaica. Hello, America."

The flight experience was breathtaking, and on top of that, I got the window seat I wanted.

We arrived in Fort Lauderdale like two hours later that day. I smelled the fresh air when I got out of the airport. I could feel the difference in the atmosphere. The climate changed and everything. I was so excited with the biggest grin on my face. That all changed when my mom told me and my brother that we had to stay with one of her friend's and take the bus to Orlando, where my grandaunt would get us from there the next day. I made sure that I did not unpack anything because I didn't want to forget anything. My brother, however, looked like he was right at home. He was already sitting in front of the TV and eating the plate of food my mom's friend gave him. I, on the other hand, ate my food and went to bed because I felt tired from such a long day.

CHAPTER 7

My New Life

We arrived at the Orlando bus station about 3 p.m. the next day. After a good 10-15 minutes, my grandaunt arrived. We were so happy to see her because had been a couple of years since we saw her last. Her van door was automatic, as I realized it when I didn't touch the door and it slid open. I was amazed because I had never seen one before, only on TV. Meanwhile, my brother was on the other side of the van fighting to open the door. I started laughing at him, but my grandaunt told me to be nice and help him.

When we got to Flagler County, I stared at the palm trees and every little thing in the neighborhood. I felt alive, like I was in heaven. Everything was so clean and pretty. When we got to Palm Coast, I knew I was finally home. My grandmother pulled up into a yard and told us welcome to our new home. I got out the car and looked around. The house was so big. It was a two-story, six-bedroom house. I couldn't believe I was about to live there. When I got in the house, I was so happy to finally start my new life.

My cousin Linda was in the kitchen cooking up a storm. The scent hit me from the moment I walked in the house. I heard a scream coming my way from one of the back room. It was my little cousin Maya. She was running and screaming in excitement to see us. When she finally got in the living room where we were standing, I so happy your her. "I am so happy you're here," she said. She wrapped her arms around me so tight I felt like I couldn't breathe until she released her grip.

I assured her that I was going to be there for a long time, so she should save some of her love for another day. Still, she held on to me again.

Linda called for us to come get some food. "It is self-serve," she announced.

Everything looked and smelled so good. I was ready to eat, but after eating half the food on my plate, I was full and ready to relax. Linda then directed me to her room where I was going to be sharing room with her until her apartment papers were finalized. I didn't mind sharing because the room was big enough for both of us, and we had always gotten along. So, I settled in and unpacked my stuff from my little bag in my new room. Afterwards, I went back out to living room to catch up with my family members.

CHAPTER 8

My Rich School

Orientation for my new school was finally here. I would get to choose my classes and meet some of my teachers. However, I was upset for the first part of that day because my guidance counselor told me that I had to repeat my freshman year because my academic history was so bad. I honestly had no one to blame but myself. I should have listened to my middle school teacher school who I thought was annoying. Every time she got in front of the class, she would tell us that "time wasted cannot be regained." I heard her say it so much that I would help her finish the sentence sometimes. Facing the prospect of retention, I understood why and what she wanted us to grasp in that speech.

I had three classes that I really wanted to take: dance, culinary arts and computers. The rest of them was mandatory. As for the school itself, the cafeteria was big and very handily arranged. The courtyard was like paradise, decorated with beautiful flowers and nice lunch tables. The football field was huge, but my favorite part of the campus was the auditorium. I would be spending a lot of time in there because I had showcases and concerts that the school would host in there.

On my first day of school, I wouldn't have any new clothes. I always heard the saying that the first impression means everything, so I was worried. Linda had given me some clothes when I got there, so I would have to choose from those for school. I found a pair of jeans and a green shirt, but one big problem remained: I didn't have any shoes. My grandaunt told me that we were going to the store the next day.

We went to a store called Payless the next day, and I saw so many shoes. My grandaunt told me that I could pick out two pairs of shoes, one of which would be for church. I started murmuring under my breath, "Why do I have to go to church?" But I guess I couldn't complain since it was her money. I took back what I said when I got to her church. It was five times the size of my old church.

When I walked in for the first time, the ushers directed me to the teenage section. I was so surprised. They had games upon games and a big flat screen TV. Not to mention, there was a full basketball court outside. I really enjoyed it, for it was different but in a good way.

I got up on Monday morning for school, got dressed and walked to the bus stop. I got there just in time to see the bus coming down the street. I didn't have a chance to eat breakfast that morning, so I had to get something from the school cafeteria. My first period was English, and it was the most difficult class I ever took. After being there for like a month, I found out that science, which I hated, was easier. I told my English teacher I couldn't understand her because she was talking too fast, and to make things worse, the lesson was on Shakespeare, which was not something we covered in Jamaica. I had no clue what she was saying half the time, but I made up in my mind that I would not let it get the best of me. I kept on repeating that saying my grandfather always told me: "Good, better, best. Never will I rest until my good is better and my better best." That's what kept me going for the rest of the school year. I kept that positive mindset until I left that school, and it did pay off because my report cards had only A's and B's.

CHAPTER 9

Flashback and the Big Move

It was two years after we first arrived, and we had to move. I was far from excited because I was finally getting used to the idea of having my own room since my cousin moved out in her own apartment. My brother had been diagnosed with sickle cell and was in and out of the hospital. Sickle cell is the kind of sickness that starts off slow and then takes over the whole body, leading to other severe complications. I felt stressed out and pressured from my brother's continuous hospital visits, and my mom always asked me to do things for him. She gave him all her attention. I felt like a motherless child at times.

One day, I got up and decided to run away from home. I was running away to a safe place, the library, at the time. I never thought about the fact that when the library closed, I would have to leave, so I packed a bag with a few pieces of clothes, some food and left notes to everyone in the house. When I got halfway down the street, my little brother came after me. The only reason I went back home was because he was sick, and I knew he needed me at the time. I blamed it on my compassionate heart because I have always tried to help in whatever way I could.

"This move that my mom is taking us on sucks," I thought. We were moving to Fort Lauderdale, right back where we started when we first got to America. and for the first time my brother was on my side, trying to convince my mom of all the reasons we could come up with for why we should stay with our grandaunt in Palm Coast. She wasn't budging, though. So the decision to move was final.

When I went outside, a car pulled up in the driveway, and to my surprise, it was the same lady who was supposed to pick us up at the airport when we first came from Jamaica. I never liked her because she left us at the bus stop lingering because she was too "busy." Apparently, she had to go to church before taking us to our destination. So we almost took the bus to Palm Coast on our first day in America. Had it not been for my mom having so many friends, we would have been stranded. One of my mother's other friends picked us up from there.

My mom told us to start packing our things in the car so that we could get to Fort Lauderdale on time. I packed my suitcase that my grandaunt bought the year before when we visited Jamaica, along with some other boxes. I hugged my family before I was about to leave. I told them good-bye but that I would see them soon, knowing where I was moving to was just a couple of hours away. We got in the car after my brother finally fit his bike in the car. He insisted on carrying it in that small car.

The entire way down to Fort Lauderdale, I rode in silence. We got there about three to four hours later that day. The car pulled into an apartment building with a big sign that read: Hampton Pines. I was trying to figure out how I was going to remember my way out with so many turns to get to our apartment, but my mom said it was only because it was night time that it looked so hard to navigate, but in the daytime, I would understand it better.

My mom got out of the car first and knocked on the apartment door. A lady and three kids came outside to help us bring our stuff inside. After we finished unpacking the car, we went inside and I started to look around, counting how many rooms was in the house.

The lady introduced herself. "My name is Chambers, and this is my daughter, Elizabeth, and my two sons, Williams and Tye."

I introduced myself as well. After she told us about our sleeping arrangements, she assured us that our stay there would be pleasant.

CHAPTER 10

My First Day at H.O.C.M.

The following Sunday, I had to go to church. I didn't want to go, but I got dressed anyways. The Sunday School service started at 9:30, so I had to get up extra early. I didn't really have church clothes due to the fact that the church I previously went to allowed people to wear whatever. I didn't bother to buy anything formal except for this one black dress that my grandaunt bought me. I didn't want to wear it, so I wore a pair of leggings and a blouse.

When I got outside, I saw a grey Toyota car with a man sitting in the driver's seat and a woman sitting in the passenger seat. I had never seen them before, so I said "hello" with a half smile.

"Hi, I'm Dre," the man said with his hand extended. I shook his hand and then the same with his wife after she introduced herself as Natalie. "I'll be taking you guys to church today."

I shook my head in approval and then went back in the house to call my mother and brother. When they came outside, I got in the car. Then I saw Chambers and her kids coming too. I was confused ,so I asked, "How are they gonna fit with us?"

My mom answered, "We're going to lap up and make it work."

I said, "Okay," and moved over in the car.

After 15 minutes, the car pulled up in a parking lot of a plaza. The door that we went through had Heart of Compassion Ministry written on it. I sat in one of the chairs in the back because I never liked sitting in the front of churches. After sitting there for a while, a lady came over and hugged me. In my mind, I was like. "This lady sure is extra friendly." I thought, "Why is she hugging me? She doesn't know me." However, there was something about when she hugged me. There was a connection I felt that I couldn't explain. The crazy thing about it was that she never said a word to me.

The service started shortly after , they prayed, read the bible and did praise and worship, I felt something move in me. It was nothing like praise and worship back in Jamaica; it was better. I sang along with them for the few songs I knew, after it ended , Dre took the Mike to give the welcome and announcement, I Wanna welcome everyone to the most excited church in Fort Lauderdale ,where everybody is somebody in Jesus name and where our pastor is nun other than Pastor Sonia B. Lee. My mouth dropped.

I couldn't believe that was the same lady that hugged me from earlier. I started mumbling, "I don't care who she is. I hope she's not trying to ask me to get baptized because it's not gonna happen."

My thoughts got interrupted by Dre, who was on the mic. "Now I would like to personally welcome sister Marie and her two children. We prayed for them, and look at God, they are here today."

They claimed to pray for us, but they didn't know us. So, as usual, I zoned out to the point that I didn't even hear when they started singing to let us know to greet everyone by going around and hugging each other. I didn't know what was going on until someone reached out to hug me. The service was pretty much a big blur after that because I was still deep in thought about the church.

When I got home, I told my mom I didn't want to go back because I heard the announcement about how many times per week they were going to have church services, including Tuesdays, Wednesdays, Thursdays, Fridays, and Sundays. "Now that is way too many times to go to church," I said. "What, did they miss God the first time they went and had to go back and look for Him?"

"No, Niki, you wouldn't understand, but like the Word of God says, 'As for me and my house, we will serve the Lord.'"

"But this is not your house. You're renting, so I'm confused."

She assured me that I would understand it sooner rather than later.

CHAPTER 11

She Asked Me the Question

After my mom gave me a long speech about going to church, I didn't want to hear it anymore, so I went. On this particular Sunday, the church was worshipping in the banquet area. When it was almost over, Pastor Lee called me and another girl out. She talked to the girl first, and the young lady started crying and falling on the ground. I wondered if she wanted me to help her up because she looked as if she was dying.

After the ushers picked her up and put her to sit on a chair, Pastor Lee turned to me again. With a serious look on her face, she said, "Now you, Miss Niki, we are going to be good friends because I beat demons out of people. I do not befriend them, and you did not just come with one, you came with legions. But it'll stop tonight. See, you came in here with a look on our face like you are about to go to war with the world, but I can't do it for you tonight, God will. You have to forgive and be delivered on tonight."

I started crying because she started to tell me some things about my past that only God and I knew about.

"Yes, that's it. Let it out, Niki." She turned and said, "Come, intercessors, gather around."

She laid her hands on me and prayed for me, as did the intercessors.

When she was done praying for me, she asked me if I believed I that I was changed on tonight. I nodded my head, yes.

"Now, Niki, this walking is a process," she explained. "It does not all happen in one day, but the first step is baptism."

I dried my eyes quickly. I was no longer crying.

She asked, "Would you like to give your life to God through the process of baptism?"

The look on my face clearly said no, as she described it . She explained to me that salvation is not a forced thing and that God himself was not going to change my answer.

"You may go back to your seat," she told me. "All we can do is pray because the change begins with you."

CHAPTER 12

My Life-Changing Decision

I came home from school one day to find Pastor Lee at my house. I thought for second that I forgot my address and went to the wrong house.

"Good evening," I said and was about to walk to my room.

When she called me back, I thought, "Oh my God, she knows. She knows that i was just kissing my boyfriend in the hallway." I turned around and walked back towards her.

"Why are you in such a rush, Niki?" she asked. "Come have a seat."

I sat down.

"Niki, do you know why I am here?"

"No, pastor," I answered.

"Well, have you thought about what I asked you?"

"Yes, pastor."

"But stop right there," she interrupted. "Now you know that God has been really good to you. Even some things that you went through and didn't tell anyone about and the root of it all is the issue with your father. You refuse to forgive him for not being there for you as a child. But you have to look at it this way, many kids your age don't even have a dad or a mom and yours is still living, which is enough to give God praise."

I thought about what she said, and then it hit me, "What do I have to lose?" All my life I've been running from God, and He still protected and kept me safe. Yet, I refuse to serve him with my whole heart because I was worried about what my friends would think about me and how boys will think I'm lame. But I think this is a chance for me to put my past behind me and look forward to the future. For far too long I've been living my life on an eggshell. Now it's time, my time to soar like an eagle."

"Yes, pastor," I started crying, "yes, pastor, I will give my life to God. I want to get baptized. I don't want to wait anymore because you are the first pastor that told me the truth and not butter up my sin and try to prophesy to me just so I can join your church. You told me with a heart of compassion. Ministry is not for everyone. It is for those with a heart that is ready to be delivered and set free. I do have a lot of issues with forgiveness and love."

With that, she got up and she hugged me, and I felt it again, that connection I couldn't explain when I first met her. But now I get it, we are connected through God. I declared in my heart, "She is my spiritual mom, and wherever she goes, I will go, and Her God shall be my God."

CHAPTER 13

Life As It Is Today

I am a now 20 years old and a Christian. I got baptized, and I am proud to say that I'm a member of heart of compassion ministry. I am now living a Godly life the best way I know how. I hold several positions in my church, joining the praise team, the dance team and the choir. I am the head of the decorating committee, and I am the youth department secretary assistant I got delivered from, drinking, partying, cursing and fornication. I still have a battlefield in my mind every day. I will never tell anyone that this Christian walk is an easy one. It is very lonely, as it took me giving up old friends and some family members who don't have anything positive to say about me.

Some people may not understand the changes I have made in my life. A lot of people don't know my story, which is why they will never understand my praise. A lot of people think they have me figured out, but little do they know that I don't praise God because I want to look cute or I want to hold a microphone. No, I am a worshiper who praises God because my life depends on it. If I don't, I will fall back into a life of sin and I truly can't afford to start my journey all over again because it's like climbing a mountain. It is easy to come down but hard to go up. I reconciled with my dad, and I finally forgave him after realizing that tomorrow is not promised to anyone. And my goal and determination is to go all the way with God, no matter the obstacles in my way because God has given me the power to jump through hoops and leap over walls. He is able.

CPSIA information can be obtained
at www.ICGtesting.com
Printed in the USA
LVHW020613230920
666822LV00005B/535

9 781735 572307